Ninjas!
A Fun Guide Book For Kids Wanting To Become A Ninja

Best Selling Author

P. D. Adler

D1365290

Ninjas!

A Fun Guide Book For Kids Wanting To Become a Ninja
First Edition

#1 Best Seller on Amazon!

Published by SunVision Media
Printed in the United States of America

ISBN-13: 978-1494836702

ISBN-10: 149483670X

Learn more information or contact the author at:
http://sunvisionmedia.blogspot.com

AVAILABLE ON KINDLE DEVICES

Presented to:

From:

Date:

Table of Contents

Dedication

I dedicate this book to all of my fellow substitute teachers who are devoted and vital to the continuation of education for our children and who find teaching both enjoyable and rewarding. I want to thank my temporary students who can be frustrating and trying at times, but are always treasured. I also want to dedicate this book to everyone in my life from my parents to my wife, children, grandchildren and friends, who have made me what I am today. It's all their fault.

Guide to Becoming a Ninja Warrior

This guide is a training manual to help you become a Ninja Warrior.

Step 1 of becoming a Ninja is to learn as much about the subject as possible. This includes the history as well as the skills needed to find your path and become what you seek. The first section of this book includes the history, training, roles and weapons used by the Ninja. A true Ninja is a master of himself and his environment and you must learn before you act.

The Ninja was a very skilled and fierce warrior belonging to a secret society and were sent by their master to spy on, collect information, or to do whatever is required to their enemy. Sometimes they were sent to steal, create confusion, insight riots or even to kill. Ninjas were both male and female.

The Ninja Warrior sometimes liked to work alone and was always on the offensive. In other words they wanted to blend into their environment and be invisible. They did not want to fight, but if they had to fight, they wanted to strike first without warning. They were experts in all types of martial arts.

Special individuals were selected to be Ninjas during the feudal wars of Japan starting around 1200 A.D. These times are over and the need for the traditional Ninja is gone; however, a new Modern Ninja is still at work today.

Before we talk about you becoming a Ninja, it's important that we discuss the history of a Ninja.

History of Ninjas

It's hard to determine the exact time when the Ninja came into being because there are very few records kept of its existence. Most of what is known about the Ninja is from stories that have been told and passed down from generation to generation.

The first stories told of "nonuse" or "the art of stealth" was in Japan in 522 A.D. and it was a religion practiced by priests. These priests were not violent and were "mystics" who gathered and shared information for the ruling classes.

The priests were constantly harassed by the central government and decided they needed some way to protect themselves, so over the next 120 years the priests learned and perfected fighting skills and the art of stealth.

Civilization flourished from 794-1192 A.D. and a new class of wealthy, privileged families emerged. Each of these families wanted more power than the other and so they started to fight or feud with each other to make or destroy emperors. As the fighting became more intense they found a need for spies, informants and assassins. They would resort to any means necessary to eliminate any possible threats. The families sought out and hired the priests to train members of their family so they could learn the great fighting skills and the art of stealth that the priests had perfected. With this, the Ninja was born.

The first Ninjas were Japanese warriors who received special training and were given special duties. These trained Ninjas worked under their leader usually to gather information, to protect them and their properties and sometimes to kill their enemies.

Since Japanese believe that Ninjas had some special magical powers that helped them fly, they were considered more than a normal human being. No wonder the Ninja is nearly considered a superman in the history of Japan.

It is also said that Japanese has a myth about the Ninja. They believed that Ninjas emerged from demons that were half man and half crow. The Ninja was originally known as Shinobi in Japanese language.

The Difference Between a Samurai and a Ninja

Samurais and Ninjas have been a part of the Japanese culture for a long time. Although both Japanese samurai and ninjas may seem alike, their differences are great. Both were widely used in Japanese history but for completely different reasons; however, both the history of the samurai and of the ninja comes from one story. A man named Prince Yamato disguised himself as a woman and lured two men who let their guard down. After they were comfortable Yamato murdered both men with a sword. While a ninja or samurai usually do not dress in a female disguise they both recognize the actions of Prince Yamato to be the start of their warrior ways.

A samurai warrior is of an elite class established in the Japanese military around 794 A.D. These men were regarded above all other warriors in Japan's culture because of the samurai's strict devotion to a high code of honor called the Bushido, being completely loyal to their master, typically a high government official. The samurai is different from a ninja because a ninja is a low class fighter paid for by anyone who could hire them.

The Samurai was expected to fight according to their rules. On the other hand, Ninjas didn't have to stick to such formalities. They were free to work as they pleased in order to achieve the results. This is why their way of carrying out the fight did not match with each others standards.

Both the samurai and the ninja were experts with different Japanese weapons. The samurai was skilled in using the spear, bow and arrows, and the sword named for these warriors, the samurai sword. It was known that a samurai was used for quick and effective hand to hand combat with any weapon available. A ninja however, used different forms of attack. They performed their duties in secret, and were better known for sneaking up on someone for a surprise assassination, or having great espionage skills.

Naturally, since the warriors had different assignments and different methods of carrying out these assignments, their clothing was also different. A samurai, as a high class warrior, wore full body suits of armor made out of metal plates covering their legs, their arms, and torso, with a metal helmet as well. Because a ninja was meant to be kept secretive, these men wore disguises that allowed them to fit into any situation. Sometimes they wore an outfit that was all black covering their legs arms, and even their head, all that was intended to show was the eyes of the ninja. Their coverings were meant to help hide them in at night. Some also believe that the ninja was fully covered because they were not a high class mercenary, like a samurai, and they did not need to be seen.

The samurai and ninja are different on most levels. Each was used in a different form of attack, dressed differently, and were of different classes. Yet the beliefs of both seem to stem from one man's historical action.

Summary:

- Both samurai and ninjas were warriors for hire. A samurai was of an elite class and the ninja was considered of a lower class.
- Both samurai and ninja recognize the historical tale of Prince Yamato at the beginning of samurai and warrior ways.
- Samurais were different in a way that they had rules for fighting. For the Ninja there were no boundaries and principles. Ninjas were dangerous and could not be controlled.
- The samurai utilized weapons in hand to hand combat, including the samurai sword. The ninja preferred to use a sneak attack on his opponents, but would use smaller weapons like the ninja star.
- Samurai wore metal clad suits of armor. Ninjas wore black outfits of cloth covering all but their eyes or other disguises to fit in.

The First Ninja Schools

Where were the first Ninja schools located?

A province is a territory and a territory is a region or large geographical area. In the early history, Japan was made up of many territories or regions which were divided by mountain ranges, rivers or other markings. Each territory was called a province. Many villages of common families lived there under the control of a ruler who oversaw everything. Some of these rulers could be brutal and were always feuding or fighting other provinces.

Around 680 A.D. the Iga and the Koga provinces broke free and each formed their own republic. They were located side by side and were separated by a mountain range.

The people who lived in the Iga province were known as the Iga Clan and the people who lived in the Koga province were known as the Koga Clan. It was here in these two provinces where villages became devoted to the training of Ninjas first appeared.

These two clans of Ninjas had different killing, spying, and attacking methods and were the best known Ninja clans in Japan.

The Koga and Iga occupied the same mountain range, in two valleys divided by a mountain and were not easy to get to because of the poor conditions of the roads. This helped keep the training of Ninjas a secret. They lived as farmers and had knowledge about medicines, herbs, weather, and agriculture.

These two clans were rivals and adopted different ethics. The Iga Clan relied on the government for their survival and adopted the Buddhist ethics while the Koga Clan remained true to their beliefs of purity.

Many famous Ninjas came from one of these two provinces and they were actively hired by very powerful territorial lords because of their great skill. The most famous and greatest Ninja, Hattori Hanzo, was a member of the Iga Clan.

Around 1581 a great War Lord named Oda Nobunaga invaded the Iga province and wiped out the organized clans. Oda Nobunaga was said to have conquered a third of Japan. When the Iga Clan was wiped out, the survivors fled to another great War Lord named Tokugawa Leyasu (who later became the commander in chief who united Japan). Hattori Hanzo was also a Samurai who saved the life of Tokugawa Leyasu and helped him come to power.

Training in the Art of Ninjutsu

For a period of time the Ninja disappeared from the scene. But sometime in the 17th or 18th century they reappeared with more in numbers. They actually exercise a variety of practices and these practices were known as Ninjutsu.

Ninjutsu is the ancient art of the Ninja shadow warriors of Japan. It is a unique method of moving and thinking which developed a system often referred to as the art of winning.

The art of Ninjutsu is best connected with the Ninja's. They are well known all around the world, for their stealth and secret life. The Ninja is known to have gone through very tough and challenging training, which hardly anyone really knows about.

At the beginning, the art of Ninja fighting was transmitted from father to son and from teacher to the best students. After some time schools were established with the specific purpose of training Ninja Warriors. Children at a very early age were sent to train and it was not uncommon for them to spend up to 20 to 25 years at the school perfecting their skills.

In those schools the students were trained to become experts. They were taught body skills, karate, spear fighting, blade-throwing, use of fire and water, defenses, and about destructive and toxic poisons. They were very smart and could move around quickly without being noticed. They learned and developed swimming, acrobatics and climbing skills. Some say they even knew how to fly short distances.

A lot of physical training was also involved. For example, during training they used rice bags and lifted them with one hand for strength and ran backwards and sideways at great speeds.

Spiritual training was taught as well as instructions in the Chinese Yin and Yang philosophy, Buddhism, herbal medicine, psychology, astronomy and magic. It was believed that this spiritual training by the Ninja gave them the power to disappear.

Roles of the Ninja

The Ninja did not always dress in the black clothing that is traditionally thought of when you think of a Ninja. If they dressed in black it was to blend into the night. Sometimes they even wore all white clothing. The primary role of a Ninja was to gather information and to do that without being caught they change their looks to create confusion. They usually appeared as very common people of everyday life like monks, priests, street performers, fortune tellers, and merchants to trick their enemies.

Roles of the Ninja:

- Espionage or the act of spying
- Sabotage or the act of destroying their enemy's camp, food, tools, weapons, or just about anything to create confusion
- Assassins, or to kill their enemy
- To fight if needed

Ninjas never worked without planning. If anyone attacked them suddenly they did not run away. They were always ready to fight like a hero. Fighting was the last resort and sometimes if they were planning an attack, they would plan the attack in numbers rather than alone.

Ninjas did not always work alone. When needed they planned and worked in a group, which was safer to trap and catch their target more easily or to complete their mission.

In battle, Ninjas were always prepared for multiple situations and events that could occur. The Ninja carried many weapons and tools that allowed them to climb walls, enter buildings, kill their enemy and escape if necessary.

Ninjas were also very careful not to be detected. It has been told that they sometimes used wooden shoes with animal footprint shapes on them so they would not leave any human tracks to be followed.

Weapons of the Ninja

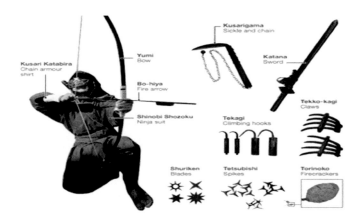

The Ninja Clans of Japan were famous for their massive arsenals of unusual weapons. Whether on an assignment of espionage, assassination, or open fighting, the Ninja Warriors had a lot of devastating devices they could use to escape, silence, wound, or even kill an enemy.

The Ninja combined and developed the use of Ninja sickles, canes, grapnels, poisons, spikes, swords, heavy weighted chains, cleated weaponry, and firearms. These weapons could be classified into five groups. These weapons would help the Ninja:

- Become invisible.
- Climb.
- Become air borne, to fly or jump far.
- To become elusive, unpredictable, and even supernatural.
- To kill.

Ninjas were very clever and are super spies because of the skill in using the tools and weapons they made. The inventive and deadly weapons created by them are viewed as some of the best weapons to this day.

Because there were so many differences in the weapons used by the Ninja clans that lived in the isolated areas of Japan, it would be difficult to include every weapon developed; however, the most popular weapons can be linked to the five groups listed above and this will give you an idea of the many types of unique weapon-tools that the Ninjas used.

Among the weapons used by ninja were knives and swords, Ashiko (spiked metal claws), different kinds of deadly Shuriken (throwing knives), and Chigirki (long straight stick with a 2-1/2 chain attached with a ball with spikes)

Shuriken were often tipped with poison. They hit them on the head of the enemies. They are heavier than you think and throwing them is not as easy as it appears in the movies.

The Ashiko were spiked claws that were worn on the feet. This helped Ninja climb faster and to harm their enemies if required.

Along with weapons other devices were also used. For example, they used special pipes to listen to conversations in nearby rooms, bamboo sticks for climbing walls as quick as cats, and smoke mixed with poison to make breathing difficult for their enemies.

They also were said to possess supernatural powers. Some include invisibility, flight, shape shifting, the ability to "split" into multiple bodies, and the skill to gather and control animals.

NOTES

_____

_____

_____

_____

_____

The Modern Ninja

In more recent times, the Ninja has become popular all over the world through cartoons, comics, and films. They are shown wearing classy black tights, juggling knives, and cracking jokes.

To many, they are fascinating real-life heroes, but in reality, they are more than that. They are very dangerous and are hired to perform dangerous acts. Sometimes their fighting is uncontrollable and they will harm whoever gets in their way. Ninjas are believed to still be around today.

There are millions of people who practice many forms of martial arts and consider themselves to be a modern Ninja; however, martial arts is only one part of being a Ninja. Remember, Ninjas only fought if necessary, but were very skilled and capable of fighting when needed.

The closest to an actual Ninja of early history can be found in the armed forces around the world. Almost all major nations have some sort of Special Forces Group. Some of these are:

From the United States

- SEALS
- RANGERS
- GREEN BERETS
- HALO Teams

From Great Britian

- SAS
- SBS

From Canada

- Z GROUP

From Russia

- SPETSNAZ

From Israel

- Mossad

The Ten Steps To How To Become A Ninja

Most people want to become or be like a Ninja in some form or another. Why not? They were and are the symbols of determination, strength and courage in the face of danger. We want to become a Ninja because we too wish to have the amazing abilities and skills related to the old Ninja.

Here are ten steps to help you on your journey to become a Ninja:

Step 1 - Learn the Ninja way

- Decide upon a series of principles, standards, and beliefs that you truly can live by.
- Educate yourself on the history of the Ninja. You have taken a big step today by reading some of the history of Ninjas. If you want to become a Ninja, or anything else, you must be an expert in the subject. Learn all you can about your subject.
- At the same time do well in school. The most successful Ninjas were smart and studied a lot.

- The Ninja lifestyle was diverse. You need to direct your lifestyle accordingly.

Step 2 – Keep it to yourself

- If you want to live like a Ninja you must keep it to yourself. Ninjas lived in secrecy. Don't tell anyone, don't brag and be private with your decision.
- Be a master spy and keep everything secret.
- Don't dress like a Ninja you see in the movies. Most Ninjas dressed like everyone else to blend-in.
- Don't think you can do everything. Being a Ninja takes time. Don't do anything crazy like jump off of buildings and don't get into fights. Remember, the Ninja's primary goal is to gather information and only fought as a last resort.
- Be noble and help people. If you see one of your classmates being picked on by other kids, stick up for him or her and help them.

Step 3 - Exercise daily

- Do pushups, sit-ups and chin-ups. Do as many as you can and try to add at least one more each week.
- Run the same distance every day and time yourself. Try to beat your time each day or each week.
- Swim as often as you can and again time yourself for each lap or distance you go. Try to move through the water as silently as you can.
- Be flexible. Do stretches and gymnastics. You can even try climbing trees or ropes.

Step 4 – Learn to move like a Ninja

- Ninjas moved in silence and tried to become invisible.

- Do not stand out in the crowd, do what everyone else does and don't attract attention.
- Learn how to escape. Know where your exit points are in every situation so you can leave without anyone knowing. You must also learn how to create a diversion if needed and remember not to leave anything behind.
- Practice sneaking up on a dog or cat.

Step 5 – Learn how to influence people

- There are many books you can read about this and become a master at it.
- Master self-control. You cannot master or control others unless you can control yourself.

Step 6 – Exercise your mind and your body

- You need to be agile and swift and you can't do that if you are out of shape. Besides regular physical exercise, yoga is a good practice to learn.
- Be very knowable about the situation you may find yourself in before going there.
- Practice to keep yourself calm by meditating.
- Sharpen your memory skills.
- It takes more than skill and ability to become a Ninja. There must be some form of purpose and ethics that govern your actions.

Step 7 - Have a Purpose and Ethics

- Ninjas served many different purposes:
    - Some for vengeance
    - Some for peace
    - Some abused their skill and abilities and became thieves

- Decide your ethics and purpose.
- Know yourself and what you stand for.

Step 8 – Learn how to fight

- Ninjas were experts in fighting and used it if necessary. Remember, their primary mission was to collect information without being seen. If they were to fight then they would be discovered.
- You can start out slow and take classes in judo then progress up to other more combative styles of fighting if desired.

Step 9 – Make a choice

- Make the choice to become a Ninja.
- Simply by choosing to become a Ninja and embracing the purpose and philosophy and train hard, do you become a Ninja.
- You must have the will to survive.

Step 10 – Practice, Practice, Practice and think like a Ninja!

USE THE NINJA CODE TO FIND YOUR NAME

A-ka	J-zu	S-ari
B-tu	K-me	T-chi
C-mi	L-ta	U-do
D-te	M-rin	V-ru
E-ku	N-to	W-mei
F-lu	O-mo	X-na
G-ji	P-no	Y-fu
H-ri	Q-ke	Z-zi
I-ki	R-shi	

Your Name:

Sadie

Ninja Name:

te rim ru

NOTES

Conclusion

"Do or do not. There is no try." -Yoda

It is a long road to becoming a Ninja. Remember it took over 100 years for the priests to master the art. You should not expect to become a Ninja in a week, month, or a year. You must have patience and master your art. Early Ninjas started as children and spent decades devoted to practicing the art and then still continued to learn to master each part or step of the Ninja to get better. Finally, I can't emphasize enough that ethics, purpose and training are crucial to becoming a Ninja so let's agree not to harm another individual, damage their property or steal. Have honor!

Read More From P. D. Adler

Thank you for buying and reading this book. I hope you have enjoyed reading it as much as I have enjoyed writing it for you. I am also writing several other beginning reader books and those books as well as any new releases can be found on my website: http://sunvisionmedia.blogspot.com/

The Adventures of Naughty Nico Series:

Fun at the Auction

The Man From Mars

The Girl Next Door

Action on the Roof

FREE EBOOK

I also enjoy interacting with my customers and if you have any comments or would like to contact me, please use my email address, padler@gmail.com. I try to personally answer every email within 24 hours.

Sincerely,

P. D. Adler

About the Author

Phillip D. Adler was born and grew up in a little town in southwest Michigan. He received his Bachelor's degree in the Air Force while taking night classes and then quickly realized that he enjoyed teaching, so he took advanced courses in literature and education as part of his Master's program from Troy State University. After retiring from 20 years of service and then a second career with surgical medical device companies as a sales representative and as a professional trainer he enjoyed many years as a substitute teacher for mostly Elementary and Middle Schools. He is semi-retired in south Florida. He is the father of two sons and grandfather of 4 children. He writes children's books about his passions and early experiences as a child, experiences he is now having with his grandchildren and experiences with students. He has several short books he is working on, some educational nonfiction books for Middle School aged children as well as some fictional children's books soon to be released.

Made in the USA
Middletown, DE
02 September 2017